COLONIAL TIMES

BY JERI CIPRIANO

Table of Contents

CHAPTER 1

COLONIAL TIMES

Colonial times started in 1607, when people from England crossed the Atlantic Ocean to set up an English **colony** in what is now Virginia. They named it "Jamestown" after James I, the king of England. Soon, more Europeans crossed the ocean to the "New World" and settled colonies. Some came to start businesses. Others, like the **Pilgrims**, came for the freedom to practice their religions.

Jamestown, in Virginia, was the earliest permanent English settlement in North America.

THE THIRTEEN COLONIES

Thirteen English colonies were founded during the colonial period. Although they were thousands of miles from England, they were still under British rule.

On July 4, 1776, representatives from the thirteen English colonies signed the Declaration of Independence. After the colonists won the American Revolution, these colonies became the original thirteen states in the United States of America.

COLONY	FOUNDED
Massachusetts	1620
Rhode Island	1636
Connecticut	1635
New Jersey	1660
Delaware	1638
New Hampshire	1623
New York	1613
Pennsylvania	1681
Maryland	1634
Virginia	1607
North Carolina	1663
South Carolina	1663
Georgia	1733

Colonial times lasted from 1607 to 1783. In some ways, life then was similar to life today. Families lived together in homes, children went to school, and people worked for a living. But in other important ways, colonial life was very different from modern life.

3

AT HOME

Life in colonial times was busy. People had to build their own houses, grow their own food, and make their own clothes and other things, including soap and candles.

Many colonists had large families. In some families, there were as many as ten or fifteen children. Just about every member of the family worked. Even children as young as six years old had chores to do, such as gathering berries or firewood.

This is an example of a colonial house.

This colonial woman is reading a book as she spins cloth to make clothes for her family.

In colonial times, many homes had a room called the **keeping room**. This room was the busiest place in the house. It was also the warmest. There was a large fireplace used for heat and for cooking. At night, the older children climbed into the attic to sleep.

← A colonial woman works in her kitchen while her children do chores.

These colonists are harvesting their crops. →

Meals had to be made from scratch. Bread had to be baked. Butter had to be churned. Chickens or pigs had to be killed and cleaned before they were cooked.

SNACK TIME

Snickerdoodles were a popular colonial cookie. People still make them today. Try this modern recipe for snickerdoodles at home.

You'll need:

1 cup shortening	1 ½ cups sugar
2 eggs	1 teaspoon vanilla
2 ¾ cups sifted flour	2 teaspoons cream of tartar
1 teaspoon baking soda	½ teaspoon salt
2 tablespoons sugar	2 teaspoons cinnamon

- Stir the shortening and sugar together in a bowl. Add eggs and vanilla.
- In separate bowl, sift together the flour, cream of tartar, baking soda, and salt.
- Combine flour mix with shortening mix. Chill for ½ hour. Shape dough into walnut-size balls and roll in mixture of sugar and cinnamon. Place 2 inches apart on ungreased sheet. Bake at 400° Fahrenheit for 7-8 minutes or until lightly browned but still soft.

Native Americans taught the colonists how to plant corn and how to cook it. Every household had dozens of corn recipes. The people also planted and cooked squash, beans, and pumpkins. They learned how to get maple **sap** from maple trees. Then they made maple sugar and maple syrup to sweeten their food.

The men and boys fished. Often, they'd hunt wild turkeys, rabbits, or deer. Some families raised chickens and hogs so that they could have eggs and meat.

This colonial woman tends her family's farm animals.

A colonial girl helps her family by peeling apples.

The colonists had to work hard when the weather was warm so that they would have enough food during the cold winters. Families smoked or salted meat. They peeled, sliced, and hung up fruits to dry. There were not many cows in early colonial days, so there was not much milk. Many people drank **cider** made from apples and other fruits.

A HOW-TO GUIDE FOR COLONIAL LIVING

The Country Housewife, a book first published in London, gave instructions for preparing meats, growing and preserving vegetables, and brewing beer and ale. Many colonists brought this book with them from England when they moved to the colonies.

These men are shearing sheep to collect wool.

This colonial family works together to spin wool into cloth.

People raised sheep for wool. First, the wool had to be shorn, or cut, from the sheep. Then it was carded, or combed, before being spun into cloth on the spinning wheel. Young girls learned how to weave wool into cloth. Women dyed the cloth different colors by using the juices of wild berries. Then they cut and sewed the cloth to make clothing.

CHAPTER 3

AT SCHOOL

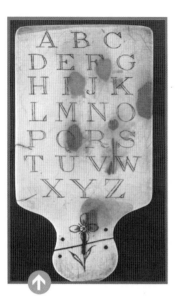

a colonial hornbook

Not all children went to school. Those who did started in what was called a **dame school**. The teacher of a dame school was a woman. Children went to her house to learn to read and write. Because books were very expensive, young children often learned their letters from a **hornbook**. A hornbook was a piece of wood with the alphabet on one side and usually a story on the other side. When children could read on both sides of the hornbook, they were finished with dame school.

This drawing shows a New England common school during the 1700s. The entire school was one room.

Towns with more than fifty families were required to build **common schools** so that boys could continue their education. In some colonies, girls could attend common school, too. In others, they stayed home and learned household duties.

Common schools had only one room. During the cold winter, a single fireplace provided the only heat. Every student had to bring in wood for the fire. If a student did not bring wood, he had to sit far from the fire's warmth.

This painting shows a New England dame school in the 1700s. The children are practicing writing their letters.

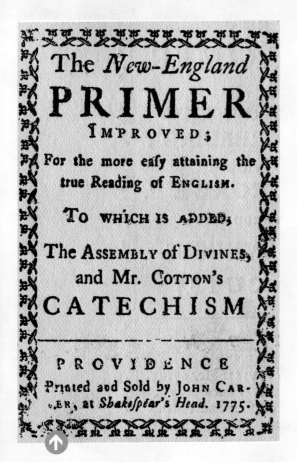

There was only one schoolbook—the New-England Primer.

The common-school teachers were usually men. Students' families were responsible for paying the teacher, who was called the schoolmaster. Some families paid with money. Others paid with food supplies.

The only schoolbook was called the *New-England Primer*. It used prayers and rhymes to teach the letters of the alphabet.

Paper was expensive, so the students wrote on peelings of birch bark. They wrote with lumps of lead or used goose-feather pens dipped in homemade ink.

quill pens and inkwells

Harvard University in Massachusetts was founded in 1636.

The boy standing in the corner (top right) is wearing a dunce cap.

Schoolmasters were strict. If a student wasn't paying attention, the schoolmaster might hang a sign around his neck that read "Idle Boy." A student who didn't know his lessons would have to sit on a dunce stool and wear a dunce cap.

At the age of eleven, when most boys finished their studies, they went to work. However, boys from wealthy families often had private tutors and went to college.

THINK IT OVER

How would you feel if you had to sit in school wearing a dunce cap? Write about it.

CHAPTER 4

AT WORK

Factories and shopping malls did not exist in early colonial times. Instead, individual **craftspeople** made and sold furniture, tools, and utensils.

Wheelwrights made and repaired wooden wheels.

Glassblowers make a variety of glassware.

This blacksmith is shoeing a horse.

People in colonial times used horses to get around. As a result, just about every town had a blacksmith who could make iron shoes for the horses. He made pots, pans, tools, and nails as well. Sometimes, the blacksmith also served as the town's dentist. He cured toothaches by pulling out teeth. Barbers often acted as dentists, too.

This colonial cobbler makes shoes at his outdoor workshop.

These coopers are making barrels in Jamestown.

When they were not riding their horses, people in colonial times walked from place to place. All of this walking was hard on their shoes. But the town **cobbler** was there to help. He repaired old shoes and made new ones.

The **cooper** was another important worker in town. The cooper made barrels and buckets. People needed barrels to store their cider, beer, and water. They also used barrels and buckets to store their salted meats and fish.

These brickmakers are busy shaping bricks and placing them in the sun to dry.

People needed homes to live in, and these were made with bricks and wood. Brickmakers and carpenters were important craftspeople in a town.

This carpenter is making doors for a new house.

IT'S A FACT!

In colonial times, both shoes in a pair were exactly the same. There was no such thing as a right shoe and a left shoe.

There were very few banks in colonial times. Instead, most people brought their silver coins to the silversmith. The silversmith melted the coins and hammered them into beautiful silverware.

Colonial silverware made from coins.

PAUL REVERE

Most people have heard of Paul Revere's famous ride to warn the colonial army that the British were going to attack. Did you know that Revere was also an expert silversmith? Some of his silverware can be seen in museums today.

A colonial town crier announces the news as townspeople listen.

There were few newspapers in early colonial times. Instead, most towns had a town crier. The town crier's job was to walk through the streets calling out the news of the day. For very special news, the town crier would bang on a drum or ring a bell. Then people would run to hear what he had to say.

People also got news from travelers who talked about what was going on in their hometowns.

THE TOWN WATCHMAN

It was against the law to be out at night. If someone was out after dark, the town watchman would send the person home. The town watchman was also a "human alarm clock." He woke up people who needed to get an early start for a long trip.

BENJAMIN FRANKLIN

Many people know that Franklin was a famous statesman and an inventor. But Franklin also helped to improve postal service in the colonies. As Postmaster of Philadelphia, he helped to cut in half the time it took to receive mail. In 1775, he was appointed Postmaster General of all the colonies.

There was no regular mail service in the colonies. It could take a month or two for a letter to reach someone in another colony. Roads and weather conditions were often bad. Sometimes, it was faster to send a letter to England! Ships carried mail to England in a few weeks' time.

In 1672, more than fifty years after the Pilgrims landed on Plymouth Rock, the first mail service began. Mail was carried by men on horseback. They were called post riders.

NEWS! NEWS!!

AARON OLIVER, *Post-Rider*, WISHES to inform the Public, that he has extended his Route; and that he now rides thro' the towns of *Troy, Pittstown, Hoosick, Mapletown,* part of *Bennington* and *Shaftsbury, Petersburgh, Stephentown, Greenbush* and *Schodack.*

All commands in his line will be received with thanks, and executed with punctuality.

He returns his sincere thanks to his former customers; and intends, by unabated diligence, to merit a continuance of their favours.

O'er ruggid hills, aud vallies wide,
He never yet has fail'd to trudge it;
As steady as the flowing tide,
He bands about the NORTHERN BUDGET.
June 18, 1799.

A post rider announces that he has extended his route.

This young girl learns the craft of spinning from her mother.

Colonial workers did not learn their skills in school. Craftspeople learned their trades by working as helpers, or **apprentices**, to other craftspeople. Young girls and boys became apprentices between the ages of ten and fifteen.

Boys were apprenticed to craftsmen, such as wheelwrights and coopers. Often, boys learned the trades of their fathers. Girls learned domestic crafts, such as weaving, candle making, and spinning. They seldom worked outside the home.

Pilgrims at Plymouth
Colony attend
Sunday worship. →

In exchange for training, apprentices worked long hours without any pay for as long as seven years. At the end of that time, each apprentice had to produce a finished object. The object was called a **masterpiece** because it was judged by the master craftsperson. If it was well made, the apprentice became a **journeyman**. Journeymen traveled from town to town repairing and making goods until they had saved up enough money to open their own shops.

This master potter works as his apprentice looks on.

People worked six days a week. On Sundays, everyone went to the meetinghouse for prayer. No one minded if a baby fell asleep during a sermon. But the church watchman made sure that no one else did.

The watchman had a long pole with a furry squirrel tail on one end and a wooden knob on the other. The watchman used the furry tail to tickle the nose of any older person who fell asleep. He used the wooden knob to wake up sleeping children by tapping them on the head. Those caught smiling or whispering in church had to pay money.

AT PLAY

In colonial days, people believed that work was good. They believed that it was a sin to be lazy.

Even so, colonial people did find some time to have fun. They shared meals with family and friends.

They celebrated important events such as holidays, weddings, a good harvest, or the completion of a new home.

Colonists dance at a wedding celebration.

↑

Some wealthy colonists dance a minuet at a friend's home.

← **A family in New England invites friends over for a meal.**

Although most colonists had little time for relaxing, some wealthier colonists did. They enjoyed tea parties, dances, and other social events.

A young girl rolls a hoop. An extra hoop could usually be found at the cooper's workshop.

This boy is playing with a ball and cup.

wooden top

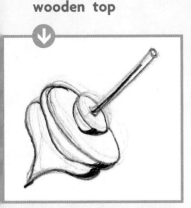

cornhusk doll

needlework sampler

Colonial children worked hard, too, but they also found ways to have fun.

Boys climbed trees and flew kites. They played with leather balls filled with feathers. They carved objects out of wood with pocketknives.

Girls played mostly with dolls. They made their own dolls from rags or from cornhusks, the leaves that cover an ear of corn.

Children sang songs, rolled hoops, and went horseback riding. They played games like tag, hide-and-seek, and charades—a game in which they acted out words for other players to guess.

COLONIAL HALL OF FAME

H ere are some important people who lived in colonial times:

William Penn

William Penn founded the colony of Pennsylvania. Penn was a **Quaker**. Quakers believed in equality. The government Penn set up was the most democratic of all the colonies.

Roger Williams

Roger Williams was an English minister who came to Boston in 1631. He founded the colony of Rhode Island so that people could practice whatever religion they wanted.

Pocahontas

Pocahontas was a Native American who helped colonists at Jamestown. She married John Rolfe and was treated like royalty by the king when she visited England.

William Bradford

In 1621, William Bradford became the first governor of Plymouth colony. He was re-elected thirty times!

George Washington

George Washington was the commander-in-chief of the Continental Army during the American Revolution. He became the first president of the United States.

Phillis Wheatley

Phillis Wheatley was brought from Africa as a slave. She taught herself Latin and English and wrote poetry that was admired by the people of her time.

CHAPTER 7

COMPARING COLONIAL AND MODERN TIMES

The customs and habits of people living in the United States today have changed in many ways since colonial times. Still, some things have remained the same. Make a chart like the one below to compare your way of life to the colonial experience you've just read about. How is it similar? How is it different?

COLONIAL LIFE	MY LIFE
AT HOME grow food, make clothes, do many chores	AT HOME buy food, buy clothes, do a few chores
AT SCHOOL	AT SCHOOL
AT WORK	AT WORK
AT PLAY	AT PLAY

GO TO →

You can learn even more about colonial life by visiting Plimoth Plantation, the site of the Mayflower Pilgrims' first settlement, online at www.plimoth.org

GLOSSARY

apprentice	(uh-PREN-tis) a person who works without pay in order to learn a trade
cider	(SY-der) juice pressed from apples
cobbler	(KAH-bler) someone who makes and repairs shoes
colony	(KAH-luh-nee) a group of people who settle in a distant land but are still under the rule of the country from which they came
common school	(KAH-mun SKOOL) a colonial one-room schoolhouse
cooper	(KOO-per) a person who makes barrels and buckets
craftspeople	(KRAFTS-pee-pul) workers who are skilled in particular trades
dame school	(DAME SKOOL) the home of the woman who teaches the youngest children
hornbook	(HORN-book) a piece of wood that has a child's first lessons written on it
journeyman	(JER-nee-mun) a person who is just beginning to earn a living at a trade after having been an apprentice
keeping room	(KEEP-ing ROOM) the main room of an early colonial house
masterpiece	(MAS-ter-pees) the finished product that apprentices make to show they have learned a craft .
Pilgrims	(PIL-grimz) a religious group that came from England to Plymouth, Massachusetts, in 1620, in search of religious freedom
Quakers	(KWAY-ker) a Christian religious sect that believes in a plain way of life and is against violence of any kind
sap	(SAP) the juice that flows through a tree
snickerdoodles	(snih-ker-DOO-dulz) colonial cookies
wheelwright	(WEEL-rite) a person who makes spinning wheels, carts, and wagons

INDEX